This Disney Stars Annual belongs to:

Name ....

Age ....

Favourite Character

....

Disney CHANNEL STARS

EGMONT
We bring stories to life

First published in Great Britain 2010 by Egmont UK Limited
239 Kensington High Street, London W8 6SA

ISBN 978 1 4052 5244 7
1 3 5 7 9 10 8 6 4 2
Printed in Italy

Contents

Hey Y'all!

Miley's got the best of both worlds!

What's the score?

Hannah Montana is THE superstar of the moment, but she's also just plain old Miley Stewart. And that's just how Miley likes it! She gets to rock out on stage, then live life as a normal gal in high school. Perfect!

Who's in charge?

Miley's dad, Robby Ray, looks after Miley and her big brother Jackson as well as being Hannah's manager and songwriter!

Where's the party?

Miley, Jackson and their dad all live in a beach house in Malibu, California. It's a bit of a change from where they used to live in Tennessee – but California *is* where all the big stars live!

BFFs?

Miley hangs out with her best buds Lilly and Oliver, who keep her secret safe. Lilly also has her own secret identity ... Lola!

Hannah vs. Miley
Guide to Life!

Are you more like Hannah or Miley? Read the guides then make your choice!

Hannah

Dress to impress

Rock to the max!

Touring the world!

Hannah Montana

Being super-famous!

Performing rules!

Writing hit songs

Miley

Hanging with my best mates

Writing notes to friends

Gotta chillax

Love being me!

Live in my fave jeans

Can't get enough movies and popcorn!

Super Season Year Planner

You'll never be bored again with this cool year planner!

Summer

It's getting hot so why not cool off?

- Learn a new sport or outdoor activity.

- Camp out in the back garden with your pals.

Make a chilled-out fruit freeze!

Ingredients

(Serves 2)

6 strawberries
1 peeled banana
Apple juice
12 grapes

Instructions

1. Chop the fruit into pieces and freeze.

2. Once frozen, place in a blender and top with apple juice.

3. Ask an adult to help you blend until it is smooth.

4. Serve straight away in a tall glass with a straw.

Autumn

There's loads of fun to have this season!

- Make three new term resolutions, e.g. I'll always hand my homework in on time!

- Learn to knit a cute scarf for the winter.

Make a leaf collage!

1. Go for a walk and collect lots of different coloured leaves.

2. Arrange your leaves in a pretty pattern on a plain piece of paper.

3. Make sure you are happy with your design before gluing down.

Winter

Wrap up warm to enjoy these cool ideas!

- Have a cosy day under your duvet with your fave book.

- Make a snowman.

Make a winter warmer soup!

Ingredients

(Serves 4)

1 chopped onion
1 chopped carrot
1 chopped stick of celery
750g chopped tomatoes
400g canned tomatoes
1 litre chicken stock

Instructions

1. Ask an adult to help you heat the onion, carrot, celery and chopped tomatoes in a pan for 5-6 minutes.
2. Add the canned tomatoes and chicken stock and simmer for 30 minutes.
3. Mix the soup with a spoon, or put into a blender if you have one.
4. Serve in bowls.

Spring

Bounce your way out of boredom!

- Plant a vegetable patch or flowers in the garden.

- Make a note of all the wildlife you start to see around you.

Spring clean your room!

1. Label two black bags, one for rubbish and one for charity.
2. Decide what order to clean out your room.
3. Tidy and dust as you sort.
4. Leave vacuuming until the end.

Fashion Whizz!

Give Hannah three unique looks, good enough for a superstar!

Use your top styling skills, to create cute and funky designs for Hannah!

You could use stripes in your design!

Act it Out!

Take the parts of Miley, Lilly and Oliver to recreate this super scene from Hannah Montana!

The scene: Miley has just auditioned for a role in the new Rob Reiner film, and Oliver has just auditioned to perform at the school dance. They're both waiting for their phones to ring to tell them how they got on ...

Miley (holding her phone and pacing up and down): Come on, come on, come on, come on, come on, come on, come on, come on ...

Oliver (doing the same): Come on, come on, come on, come on, come on, come on, come on, come on ...

Lilly: Are we gonna spend the entire weekend waiting to see if YOU got the part or YOU got the gig?

(Miley and Oliver stare motionless at their phones)

Lilly: Wake up! Move! Do something!

(Miley and Oliver make small movements)

Oliver: There.

Miley: Happy?

Lilly: It is times like these I thank my lucky stars I have no talent.

Miley: I didn't get the part. That's why Howard hasn't called me. He doesn't have the guts. Or he's having problems with his guts and he's in the bathroom. Call!

Oliver: You know, I sang great. Mr. Meadows is just jealous. He's jealous that he doesn't have my talent. I mean, you know what they say: "Those who can't sing, teach."

Lilly: Maybe I should be a teacher!

(Suddenly both phones start to ring – ask a friend to make the noise from backstage! Miley and Oliver stare at them, unable to move)

Oliver & Miley: Oh boy, oh boy, oh boy, oh boy, oh boy, oh boy, oh boy, oh boy …

Lilly: Answer the phones!

Miley (into her phone): Yeah, I totally understand. Thanks for the call … I got a call back! I'm meeting Rob Reiner!

Lilly & Miley (jumping up and down): Whoo-hoo! Yay! Yay! Yay! Yay! Yay! Yay! Yay!

Oliver: Yes sir, I completely understand. Thanks for the call.

Lilly & Miley (jumping up and down): Whoo-hoo! Yay! Yay! Yay! Yay! Yay! Yay! Yay!

Miley: Why aren't you jumping?

Lilly: Why aren't you yaying?

Miley: Why aren't you jumping and yaying?

Oliver: I didn't get it.

Miley: I'm sorry Oliver …

Over to you!
Now it's your turn to write a script and finish the show. Will Oliver be OK? Will Miley get the role in the film? It's up to you!

What's Your Star Style?

Follow the flow to find out your result!

Start

You love to stand out from the crowd!

Totally! → **If it's got rhinestones, it's yours!**

Not in this life! →

Not really →

Oh yes! →

If you love a style you'll go for it – even if it's not in fashion!

Tassels on a leather jacket?

Kinda →

For sure! →

Got your own unique look?

Chilling in jeans and your fave top is a must!

No way!

Coo...

Not cool

Definitely!

Maybe...

Ye...

Bright colours and lots of 'em!

Dream!

Nightmare!

Sort of!

Someone disses your style. Do you care?

Nope!

No way!

Simply obsessed with fashion?

Yup!

Hannah

You're all about the glitz and glam! Well, you DO have to stand out while you're performing on stage, right?

Miley

Just like Miley, you like to blend in with the crowd and still look cool! You love your jeans and chilled out styles.

Lola

Fashion is your life! You don't care if the rest of the world doesn't quite agree with you, they will one day!

Miley's Laptop

Take a peek at Miley's laptop to figure out who her emails are from!

1

Hey! You've got mail!

To: **Miley Stewart**

From:

Hey girl! Come over later and check out my new sneakers. OMG I think I'm in love. Can you be in love with a pair of sneakers? Anyway, gotta run, see you at the concert tomorrow night ;)

Who's it from? Write their name here.

2

Hey! You've got mail!

To: **Miley Stewart**

From:

Hey Miley,
I know this is like, the millionth time of asking, but can I borrow your English notes? I got distracted in class thinking about the amazing hot dogs they have in the cafeteria!

Have you got it right?

3

Hey! You've got mail!

To: Miley Stewart

From:

Miley, stop messing about on your laptop and tidy your room like I told you. I can hear you tapping from all the way down here! Don't you have a history assignment due in tomorrow?

Oops, Miley's in trouble!

4

Hey! You've got mail!

To: Miley Stewart

From:

I'm not talking to you, so I'll have to email you instead. Did you use my hair gel again? I need it tonight for my big date! Give it back and I won't break your favourite guitar!

This guy's a bit grumpy!

Star-studded

As every girl knows, you can't be a star without some of these essential accessories. Can you find them all in the star grid?

Guitar

Microphone

Big Smile

Heels

Lip gloss

Bracelets

Nail polish

Words can read up, down, side to side, backwards, forwards and diagonally.

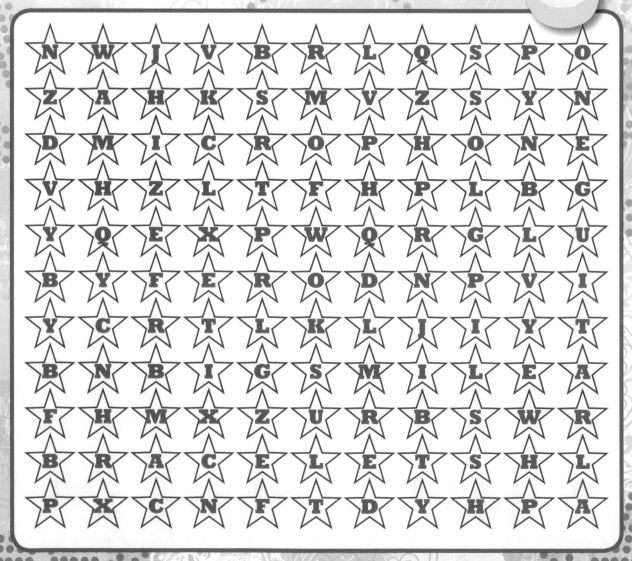

N W J V B R L Q S P O

Z A H K S M V Z S Y N

D M I C R O P H O N E

V H Z L T F H P L B G

Y Q E X P W Q R G L U

B Y F E R O D N P V I

Y C R T L K L J I Y T

B N B I G S M I L E A

F H M X Z U R B S W R

B R A C E L E T S H L

P X C N F T D Y H P A

Answers on page 67.

Guitar Match

Without her guitar Hannah feels lost. Are there enough guitars here for each Hannah to have one?

Answer on page 67.

Dancing Shoes

You know and love the song "Best of Both Worlds" and now here are some top tips for lighting up the dance floor Hannah style!

Dance Move 1: In time to the music call out: wide left, wide right, back left, back right.

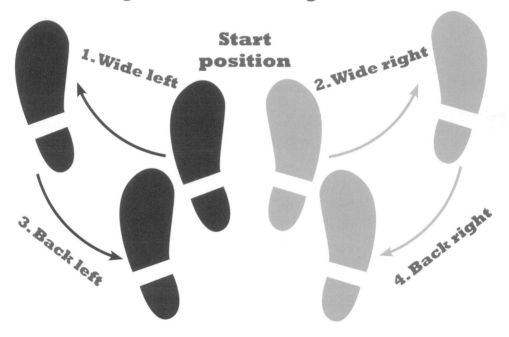

And then: wide right, wide left, back right, back left.

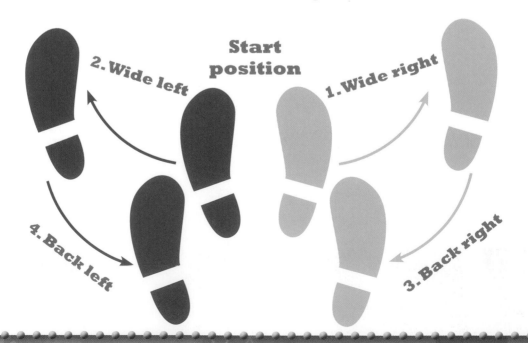

Dance Move2: In time to the music call out:
left, touch, centre, centre, right, touch, centre, centre.

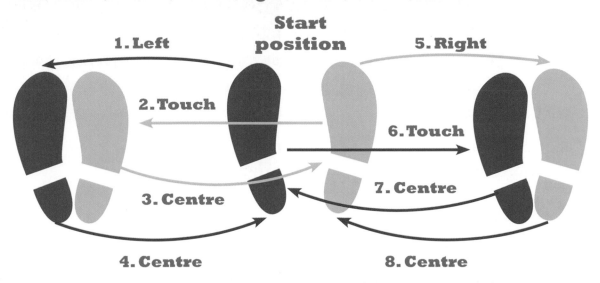

Start position

1. Left
5. Right
2. Touch
6. Touch
3. Centre
7. Centre
4. Centre
8. Centre

And while your feet are working hard, don't forget those arms.
Try some of Hannah's classic moves.

Hand in the air.

Behind your head.

To the side.

23

Miley and Lilly's School Survival Tips

Miley and Lilly are here to guide you through your day!

Circle your favourite time of the day!

8am Wake up!
Lilly: OK, this is where you get to show off the real you! Do your hair in a different way or tie your tie in a short style!

9am Maths
Miley: Your first lesson of the day! I know you haven't seen your BFF for, like, an hour but that juicy piece of gossip is going to have to wait!

11am PE
Lilly: Tricky one. You want to look good, but if you play too well the scary PE teacher might make you take part in a shot-put tournament!
Miley: Hey, that might not be so bad!

1pm Lunch
Miley: Choosing what to have for lunch is crucial! Steer clear of anything with garlic and onions – unless your last lesson of the day is vampire slaying!

3pm History
Lilly: Beat the afternoon snooze-fest by pretending your boring-old teacher is actually a top movie star. Suddenly you'll find yourself listening to everything he says!

6pm Homework
Lilly: Homework is sooo much better when I do it with my best mate, Miley.
Miley: Er, yeah, when you stop chatting and do some work!

Think You Know ... *HANNAH MONTANA* ?

Answer the questions to see how much you really know!

1. What are the names of Miley's two best friends?

2. What is Miley's biggest secret?

3. What does Miley's dad, Robby Ray, do?

4. Does Miley have a brother or sister?

5. What are they called?

6. Where do Miley and her family live?

7. Where did Miley and her family used to live?

8. What instrument does Hannah / Miley play?

9. What's the name of Lilly's secret identity?

10. What is Oliver's talent?

Answers on page 67.

Welcome to Waverly Place

The magical threesome from NYC!

What's the score?

Alex, Justin and Max Russo are three normal kids living in New York – who just happen to be wizards in training! And it's up to their dad, Jerry, to teach them the wizard way.

Who's in charge?

Jerry was once a wizard, but he gave up his powers to marry Theresa, the Wizards' human mum. They run the Waverly Sub Station restaurant!

Where's the party?

The Russos live behind the Sub Station, but if you take a step inside their freezer you'll discover the secret Lair, where Alex, Justin and Max study magic!

BFF?

Alex's best friend is Harper – she's fun, quirky and has a bit of a crush on Justin. She also doesn't have a clue that her best pal is really a wizard!

Justin

Age: 16

Biog: Justin takes his magic training very seriously. He can even bore his own dad with magical facts! He always looks after his little bro and sis – especially if they get into trouble!

Alex

Age: 14

Biog: Justin might be the oldest, but Alex is the queen of Waverly Place. She's tough, cheeky and can't wait to be a wizard full-time when she's older.

Max

Age: 12

Biog: Max loves helping out with his brother and sister's crazy plans, but his favourite thing is to invent new sandwiches for the Sub Station!

Which Wizard are You?

Find out which of the magical three you would be!

Start

Do you think magic should be used for fun or to help people?

For fun!

You've seen an outfit you really want! Would you use magic to get it?

Yes!

Er, sometimes

No way!

To help!

Always pay attention to your teacher in class?

Do you take ages deciding what to wear in the morning?

Totally!

Of course!

Not really

Giggle!

Your best friend trips in the playground. Do you giggle or go and help her?

Ever played a joke on a member of your family?

Oh yes!

Help!

Nope!

'Fashionista Presto!' would be your dream spell!

Yes!

Er, no!

Have you ever been in trouble at school?

Yes!

No!

Not really!

Do you always try to get good grades?

Yup!

Alex

You love magic, especially when it gets you what you want. You don't always listen to advice and sometimes get into trouble!

Max

Even though you're new to magic, you love playing and doing silly tricks. You like having fun and would do anything for a laugh.

Justin

To you, magic is to be learnt and used appropriately, or it could get dangerous! You play by the rules, most of the time!

Get Magical!

Wow your friends with these simple tricks!

The Money Maker

What you'll need:

- ☆ Hardback book
- ☆ Ten coins (five or ten pence pieces are perfect)

The trick!

Open a book and ask your friend to place five coins in the crease between the pages. Close the book and say the words "Coinus et doublus!" When you open the book again, your friend will be amazed to see that the coins have doubled!

The magic!

1. Before you start, hide five coins in the spine of your book. Make sure you don't pick up the book until the end of the trick or you may spoil the surprise!

2. Ask your friend to place five coins along the crease of the book.

3. Carefully close the book and say the magic words. Open the book, then tip it up so that all the coins pour on to the table at the same time.

Ta dah

The Movie Mind Game!

What you'll need:
- ☆ Paper
- ☆ Pen
- ☆ Glass bowl

The trick!
Five film names are written on pieces of paper and placed in a bowl. You will be able to predict the film name to be picked out!

The magic!
1. Ask five friends to say the name of a film out loud.
2. Write the name of the first film on a piece of paper, fold it in half and place it in the bowl.
3. Now, pretend you are writing down the name of the next friend's film, but sneakily write the first film, again.
4. Do this for each film name that is called out, so the papers are the same.
5. Ask a friend to choose a piece of paper and read it silently to themselves. Pretend to read their mind as you say the name of the film out loud!

The Number Noodle

What you'll need:
- ☆ Pen
- ☆ Calculator
- ☆ Paper
- ☆ Envelope

The trick!
Ask a friend to write down the following things in a list:
- ☆ The year they were born.
- ☆ The year of a special event in their life.
- ☆ The number of years that have passed since that date and now.
- ☆ The age they are, or will be on their birthday this year.

Add up all the numbers.
Reveal your matching prediction!

The magic!
This one's easy peasy. No matter what dates and numbers your friend thinks of, the answer will always be two-times the current year.

> **For example:**
> 2010 / 4020
> 2011 / 4022

Check out the example below and try it yourself, it really works! Before you start the trick, write the answer on a piece of paper and place it in an envelope.

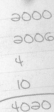

Year they were born: 2000
The year of a special event: 2006
The number of years passed: 4
The age they are or will be: 10
4020

31

Mystical Memory Spell

Take a look at the pictures below, then cover this page with a scarf or tea towel.

**Use the power of your memory
to work out which object is missing!**

Wizardly Words

Fit the words below into the grid. We've given you a few letters to get you started!

Three letters:
Mum
Dad
Max

Four letters:
Lair
Alex

Five letters:
Magic
Spell
Trick
Stars
Learn

Six letters:
Harper
Justin

Eight letters
Sandwich

Seven letters:
Trouble

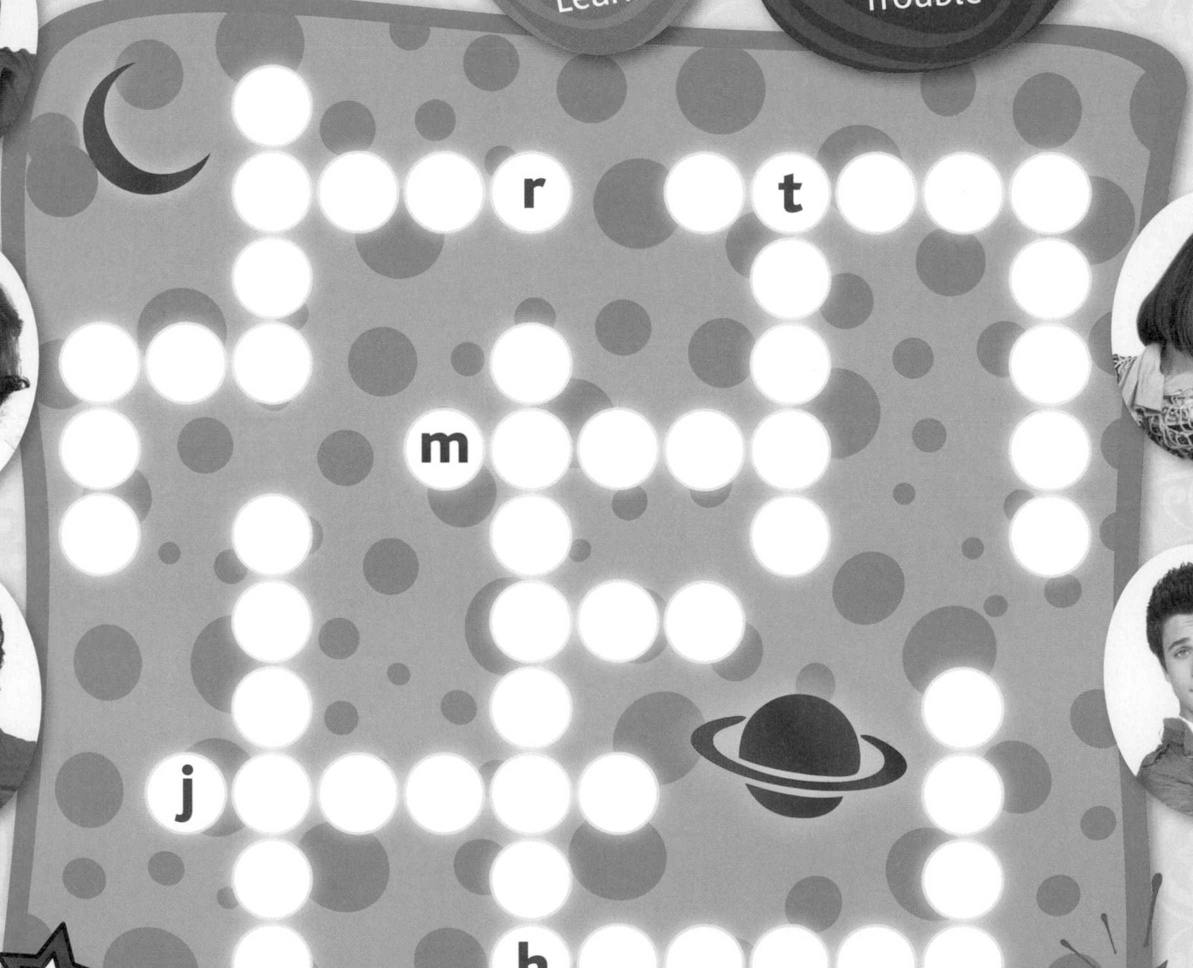

r   t

m

j

h

Answers on page 67.

Spooky Spot

Can you spot eight differences in these two pictures of the Russos' home?

Answers on page 67.

35

Cosmic Code

Life is hectic when you are a wizard in training, especially if your name is Alex. She has double booked herself again.

Help Justin decode the secret message she has sent him. You'd better be quick, otherwise there will be big trouble from Mum and Dad!

Answer on page 67.

Maze Magic

Alex has cast a spell to give herself a great new look, but she has to get back to the Lair before the magic runs out and Harper discovers her secret.

Start →

Help her through the maze. Each time she passes a magic wand she has the power to pass through one wall.

Answer on page 67.

Finish

39

Alex's Chunky Chicken Sandwich

Make a sandwich for you and a friend!

Ingredients:
Serves two

- ☆ 40g celery
- ☆ 1 tablespoon light mayonnaise
- ☆ 1 tablespoon low fat plain yogurt
- ☆ 125g cooked chicken
- ☆ 4 slices wholegrain bread
- ☆ 4 tomato slices
- ☆ 2 lettuce leaves

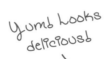

Yum! Looks delicious!

What to do:

1. Carefully chop the chicken and celery into small chunks.

2. Mix the mayonnaise, yoghurt, chicken and celery in a bowl.

3. Spread the mixture on two slices of wholegrain bread.

4. On top of each slice, place two slices of tomato and a lettuce leaf.

5. Top each sandwich with another slice of wholegrain bread.

6. Cut the sandwiches in half and they're ready to eat.

Ask an adult to help when using knives!

Think You Know ...  ?

Answer the questions to find out how much you really know!

1. What's the name of the sandwich shop owned by Alex, Justin and Max's mum and dad?

2. What's the name of the secret magic teaching area?

3. How do you get there?

4. What's the name of Alex's best friend?

5. Who does she have a secret crush on?

6. What are the names of the Wizards' parents?

7. How old is Justin?

8. In which city do the Wizards and their family live?

9. What is Alex's biggest passion (apart from magic!)?

10. What does Max love to do?

Answers on page 68.

Time to Scream!

Brothers that rock together, roll together!

What's the score?

Kevin, Nick and Joe make up JONAS, one of the **biggest bands on the planet**! They do their homework, go on tour and try to avoid **screaming fans** when putting out the trash!

Who's in charge?

Dad looks after the band and schedules the tour, while their **mum** tries to keep the boys' feet on the ground with daily chores.

Where's the party?

The guys live in an **old fire house**, which is pretty cool. When they need to get downstairs in a **flash** they slide down the **old fire poles**!

BFF?

JONAS have grown up with their best pal, **Stella**, and now she's their **fashion guru**! Plus, she's one of the only girls on the planet who **doesn't scream** when JONAS are about.

Everybody loves ... Nick!

Band credentials:
Nick is multi-talented,
he plays the drums, piano,
guitar and vocals and
is a top songwriter, too!

Biog:
Nick is the youngest member of
the group and a bit of a dreamer.
He's always falling head over heels
in love, but the real love of his life
is the band! He's kind, thoughtful
and always sees the best in people
– as well as trying to keep his
mum and dad happy!

Facts:
★ His favourite colour is electric indigo.
★ He doesn't like being treated like a baby.
★ The drum kit in his bedroom lifts up
   to reveal a cool sunken bed!

Everybody loves... Kevin!

Band credentials:

Although Kevin's official role is playing the guitar and singing, he's also great at getting his brothers to relax and have fun!

Biog:

Even though he acts a little goofy at times, Kevin is a typical older brother and keeps a watchful eye over his little bros ... as well as teasing them whenever he can! He's also a real sharp dresser and almost never wears trainers!

Facts:

⭐ His favourite snack is chocolate tacos!

⭐ He thinks his best feature is his hair!

⭐ He cries at his family's home movies – and isn't afraid to admit it!

Everybody loves...
♪ Joe! ♪

Band credentials:
Joe plays the guitar and is a cool singer, too. He's also great at spotting an opportunity to make the band even more successful!

Biog:
Joe is the true rock star of the group. He walks the walk and talks the talk and has a fondness for skinny jeans and leather jackets. Joe and Stella sometimes bicker, but secretly they have a soft spot for each other!

Facts:
⭐ He really likes keeping fit and has a mini gym in his room.

⭐ He once had a crush on a pizza delivery girl.

⭐ He's very honest – even if he sometimes says the wrong thing.

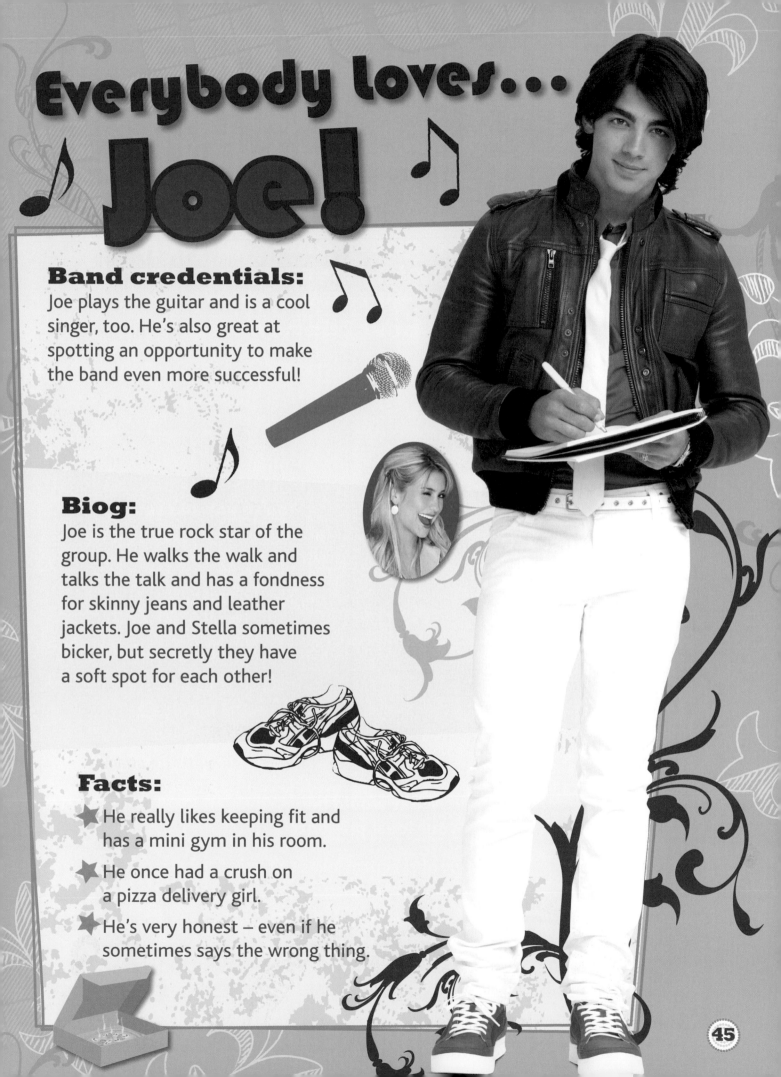

Who's Your Musical Mate?

Answer the questions, count up how many of each symbol you get and see which brother you would be best friends with!

1.

You're stuck at school with thousands of screaming fans blocking your way home. What do you do?

a. Call your helicopter pilot ◉

b. Call your mum ✳

c. Set up camp in the school gym ★

2.

You've got an evening all to yourself with no band practice! What do you get up to?

a. Stay in and catch up with fan mail ✳

b. Polish your collection of boots ★

c. Practise your rock star face in the mirror ◉

3.

What would be your ideal present?

a. A box of practical jokes to play on your brothers ★

b. A new leather jacket ◉

c. Something handmade from your best friend ✳

4.
What is your favourite type of song?

a. Songs you can rock out to!

b. Slow love songs ✿

c. Anything you can dance and jump around to! ★

5.
You've forgotten to do your homework! What's the plan?

a. Own up and take the punishment ✿

b. Make up a silly excuse ★

c. Pretend you weren't set any homework! ◎

6.
You're about to go on stage when you are struck by stage fright! What now?

a. Turn and ask your dad / manager what to do ✿

b. Run around screaming until you feel better ★

c. Stage fright? Never heard of it ... ◎

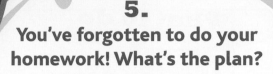

Mostly stars ...
Kevin

You and Kevin would get along really well because you're both a little goofy! You see the fun in things and couldn't be serious if you tried!

Mostly flowers ...
Nick

You're an old romantic and a home-body, too. You and Nick both think your parents' opinion is important and hate to argue with anyone!

Mostly circles ...
Joe

A rock star in waiting? Then Joe would be your perfect buddy. You love the super-cool lifestyle of being in a band and looking great 24/7!

fortune Teller

Find out your musical destiny with this cool fortune teller!

What to do

1. Cut a plain piece of paper to 20cm by 20cm.
2. Fold each corner of the page into the middle.
3. Flip it over and again fold each corner into the middle.
4. Flip it over a second time and insert your thumb and forefinger under the flaps to make the fortune teller 3D so you can open and close it!
5. Open up the fortune teller and unfold. Write on the names and numbers, as shown, then write in the fortunes, below.

   a. Lead singer in waiting!   **e.** Musical mastermind!
   b. Bass guitar is for you!   **f.** Super stylist!
   c. Little drummer girl!   **g.** Lead guitar gal!
   d. Song-writing sister!   **h.** Backing vocals honey!

6. Now close up your fortune teller again.

20cm

20cm

Nick 7 h a 8 Joe

3 4

g b
f c

2 1

Kevin 6 e d 5 Love all 3

How to play!

1. Keep the fortune teller closed, then ask a friend to choose either a member of JONAS or 'Love all 3'.

2. Spell out the chosen name or words, opening and closing the fortune teller each way as you go.

3. Now, ask your friend to pick out one of the numbers inside the fortune teller.

4. Open it up and read the fortune underneath!

49

Gig Dash!

Uh, oh! JONAS are late for a gig and they're all in different places! Can you help them get to the show on time?

What to do:

1. Choose which member you would like to be.
2. Use a coin or button as a counter and place it on your character's starting position.
3. The first person to roll a 6 starts.
4. Take turns to roll a dice. Move 2 spaces for even numbers and 1 space for odd numbers.
5. When you land on a space with writing you must do what it says.
6. The first player to reach the centre circle on an exact roll, wins!

7. You're almost there! Move on 1.

8.

6.

9. Stop to check your hair in a shop window. Go back 1.

5. Hum a JONAS tune until your next go, or miss a turn!

10.

4.

3. Name a JONAS song to move forward 1.

2.

1.

Start
Quick! Stop chatting to your pals at the school gates! You've got a gig to get to!

Kevin

Horace Mantis Academy

50

Joe

The old fire house

Start
Wake up, Joe! You've got a show tonight!

1.

2.

3. Mum makes you a snack for the ride. Go forward 1.

4.

5. Oops, you get stuck on the fire pole! Miss a go.

6.

7. You can see the show's venue! Sing the JONAS theme tune to move forward 1.

8.

9. You stop off at the gym. Go back 1.

10.

FINISH
You've made it to the show!

Nick

The mall

Start
Stop shopping and get to the gig!

1.

2.

3. Oops, you've forgotten your drumsticks! Go back 1.

4.

5. You found a short cut! Rock on 1!

6.

7. Whistle a JONAS song until your next turn or miss a go!

8.

9. You catch a lift with Dad! Dash to the gig by moving on 1.

10.

Take a Closer Look

Here's your chance to get up close and personal with JONAS. These pictures look the same but 5 things are different in picture 2. Can you spot them all?

1

2

Answers on page 68.

Screaming fans

The fans are going crazy! How many times can you find the word scream in this grid? Words can read up, down, side to side, backwards and forwards.

S	C	R	E	A	M	S	C	R	E	S
C	A	S	C	R	E	A	M	C	S	S
R	S	C	E	A	M	S	C	R	E	C
E	A	M	S	S	C	R	E	A	M	R
A	C	S	C	R	E	A	M	M	E	E
M	A	M	S	C	M	R	E	A	M	A
M	A	E	R	C	S	C	R	E	A	M
S	C	R	E	A	M	A	E	R	C	S
S	S	C	R	E	A	M	C	C	R	E
A	M	S	M	A	E	R	C	S	C	R
E	E	A	S	C	R	E	A	M	M	S	C

Answers on page 68.

JONAS Sudoku

Fill in the grid by writing in the characters' names!

Who goes here?

Make sure each person appears once in each row, column and square of 4.

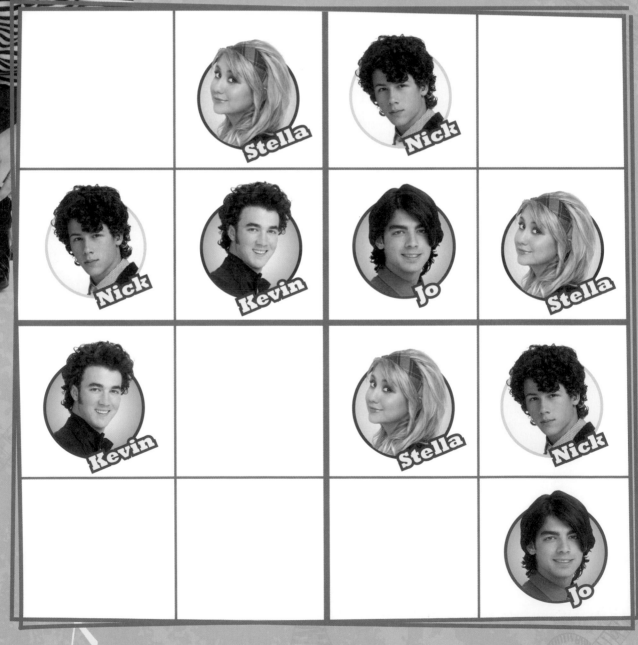

Answer on page 68.

Think You Know ... JONAS?

Answer the questions to see how much you really know about the band!

1. Whose favourite snack is chocolate tacos?

2. What's the name of the boys' best friend and stylist?

3. What does the band's dad do?

4. How do the boys quickly get downstairs from their rooms?

5. What's Nick's favourite colour?

6. Who plays the drums?

7. Where do JONAS live?

8. How do the band know Stella?

9. Where is Nick's bed?

10. What healthy thing does Joe have in his room?

Answers on page 68.

It's SO Random!

What a show and what a cast! Tonight the hit, comedy show So Random! has nominees in all the main categories at the Tween Choice Awards' ceremony. It's all thanks to the show's producer, Marshall Pike.

Best Newcomer:
Sonny Munroe

She's the new kid on the show. Her talent was first spotted by producers who saw her hilarious, self-produced internet short. Back then she was just a regular kid, living in Wisconsin, who liked to make her friends laugh. Now she's on national TV and she's funnier than ever!

Best Drama Queen:
Tawni Hart

She's been in showbiz since she was three and she's the longest running member of the So Random! cast. After her starring role in the "Drama Queen" sketch and her backstage tears and tantrums she is sure to pick up this award.

Best Goof Ball:
Grady Mitchell

This funny guy is originally from Orlando and his secret ambition is to write a comic book. Behind the scenes of So Random! he keeps everyone laughing with his practical jokes and wacky sense of humour.

Best Chilled-Out Comic:
Nico Harris

He started performing stand-up comedy when he was just five years old. Nothing gets to this guy. He has his own style, his own sense of humour and the girls love it! When the music starts, you'll find Nico on the dance floor surrounded by admirers.

Best Disappearing Act:
Zora Lancaster

She's the youngest cast member of So Random! and without a doubt the most random! She's forever popping up where you least expect to see her and she disappears equally fast. But with an IQ at genius level what else would you expect!

But much to the dismay of the So Random! cast, it's not just their show that is lapping up the awards, their rival from Mackenzie Falls is up for an award too:

Outstanding Achievement:
Chad Dylan Cooper

As a kid Chad Dylan used to write, direct, produce and star in his own home movies and ever since that time he's never stopped being a star – well in his own eyes anyway! His acting has been called wooden but with that million dollar smile there is no doubting the attention his fans pay to him – is he a heart throb or what?!

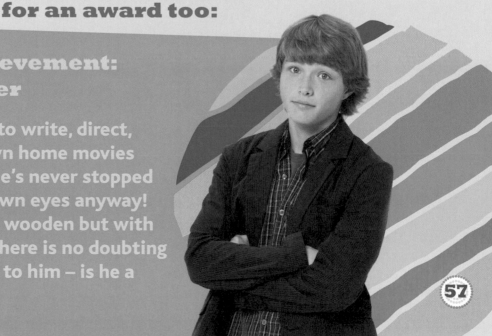

Sketchtastic!

All the cast members of So Random! are encouraged to come up with their own ideas for crazy sketches and now it's your turn. Think big laughs, think So Random! Pick from these ideas or come up with your own.

The cast:

Tawni	Nico
Sonny	Zora
Grady	You
Your best friend	
Your kid brother	

The location:

School canteen

Tropical beach

Bus stop

Pigsty

Ice rink

The costumes:

Fat suits

Seriously silly wigs

Pantomime horse

Carrot suit

Feather boas

The random prop:

Alarm clock

Tomato ketchup

UFO

Banana peel

Traffic lights

The Sketch:

58

You Must be Joking!

Sonny and the cast of So Random! Love a good joke, or a bad one! Put your funny hat on and have a go at finding the missing words in these jokes then write your answers in the grid.

Across:

1. What do cats like for breakfast?

_ _ _ _ crispies.

2. What's black and white and read all over?

A _ _ _ _ _ _ _ _ _.

3. Why did the teacher wear sunglasses?

Because her class was too _ _ _ _ _ _.

4. Why can you never play jokes on snakes?

You can never pull their _ _ _ _.

5. Doctor, _ _ _ _ _ _,
I think I'm a dustbin.

Don't talk rubbish.

Down:

1. What goes ha ha bonk?

A man laughing his _ _ _ _ off.

2. What did the traffic light say to the car?

Don't look, I'm _ _ _ _ _ _ _ _.

3. Did you hear about the leopard who had a bath every day?

He's _ _ _ _ less.

59

Forfeit Frenzy

You're late to the studio to film the next episode of So Random! The funnier you are the faster you will get there!

Start

You can play this game with a friend. You will need a dice and a counter each. You can use buttons or coins. The first person to roll a 6 starts. Take turns to roll the dice and move your counters. If you land on a forfeit, have a go at it. Miss a turn if you chicken out. Roll again if you get a laugh! The first counter across the finish line wins.

1

2
Tell a 'Knock, knock' joke.

3

4
Do a belly dance.

5
Do an impression of Tawni in a temper.

6

7

10

11 Swap socks with your friend.

12 Act like a chimpanzee.

13

Randomaniac

9 Sing 'Happy Birthday' badly out of tune.

14 Find the strangest place you can to hide, Zora-style.

8 Pretend to slip on a banana skin.

15 Do an impression of your teacher.

16

CHILLAXING ON THE SET

Finish

Fan Mail Mix-up

Now that Sonny is on national TV she gets a lot of fan mail, but the guy from the post room has mixed up the post. Can you work out who these are aimed at?

1

Dear _____

You are so dreamy, I watch your show all the time. You're such a talented actor -always so serious and intense. Please, please, please will you send me a signed photograph- I will treasure it always.

xOxOxOxOxOxOxOxOxOxO

2

Hey _____

You crack me up with the crazy costumes you get to wear. My favourite character of yours is Dolphin Boy – he's so cool. I hear that even when you're not on stage you play practical jokes and make everyone laugh – nice one!

4

Dear _____

I love your style. Everything about you just screams out showbiz glam. I hear that you have a full gym in your dressing room – how awesome, that must be how you keep in such good shape.

x x x

3

Dear _____

So Random! has got heaps better since you joined the cast. The fact that you love what you do, just shines through. Thanks for making me and my friends laugh so much each week. You're totally awesome. x

Answers on page 68.

Think You Know ...

Sonny WITH A CHANCE **?**

Answer the questions to see how much you really know!

1 Who's the youngest cast member?

----

2 Where did Sonny used to live?

----

3 What's Chad's full name?

----

4. Which cast member has the most glam dressing room?

----

5. Which character wears her hair in braids?

----

6. Who's the sportiest cast member?

----

7. What's the name of the show's producer?

----

8. What's the name of the show Sonny stars in?

----

9. Where is Grady from originally?

----

10. What's the name of the show Chad stars in?

63

Answers on page 68.

Returning Rockers

It's time to head for camp again – Camp Rock!

Yes, your favourite rockers Shane and Mitchie are back for The Final Jam.

And they're not alone ... Shane's bandmates, Jason and Nate, are joining him for the best summer ever! But this year a rival camp has opened up across the lake ...Stand back for the Camp Star v Camp Rock face off!

Shane

Mitchie

When you've finished with this annual why not cut out the page opposite. It'll make a rocking poster for your room!

I'm the Star

Now you've read all about your favourite stars, it's time to create your own show! Fill in each section then have a go at writing your very own episode!

Fill in your ideas here!

Show title

What's it all about?

Are you a secret superstar? Can you do magic? Or maybe you're just a normal gal. Your call!

What's your name?

Your character has to have a memorable name so your fans always know who you are!

Who's your BFF?

Everyone needs a best friend to hang out and share adventures with – who's yours?

Where's the party?

Where will your show be set? It could be your home, somewhere far away, or completely made up!

Answers

Find out just how well you did!

P18-19 - Miley's Laptop
1. Lilly
2. Oliver
3. Robby Ray
4. Jackson

P20

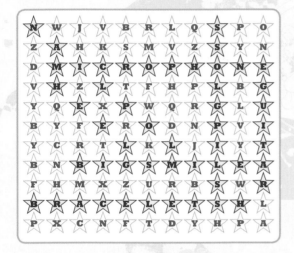

P21 - Guitar Match
No, there are 12 Hannah's and only 11 guitars.

P25 - Think You Know ... Hannah Montana?
1. Lilly and Oliver
2. She's also Hannah Montana!
3. He's Miley's manager and songwriter
4. One brother
5. Jackson
6. In a beach house in California
7. Tennessee
8. The guitar
9. Lola
10. DJing and singing

P32-33

P34-35

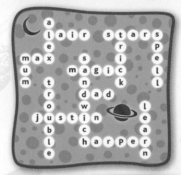

P37 - Cosmic Code
Cover for me at the Sub Station. I will make it up to you.

P38-39

67

P41 - Think You Know ... Wizards of Waverly Place?

1. The Sub Station
2. The Lair
3. Through the freezer
4. Harper
5. Justin
6. Theresa and Jerry
7. 16
8. New York
9. Fashion
10. Inventing new sandwiches

P52

P53 - Screaming Fans

The word scream appears 14 times.

P54

P55 - Think You Know ... JONAS?

1. Kevin
2. Stella
3. He looks after the band
4. They slide down the fire poles
5. Electric indigo
6. Nick
7. In an old fire house
8. They grew up together
9. Under his drum kit
10. A mini gym

P59 - You Must be Joking!

```
      M I C E
    H   H
  N E W S P A P E R
    A   A
    D   N
        G
      B R I G H T
        I
      L E G S
          P
        D O C T O R
          T
```

P62 - Fan Mail Mix-up

1. Chad
2. Grady
3. Sonny
4. Tawni

P63 - Think You Know ... Sonny with a Chance?

1. Zora
2. Wisconsin
3. Chad Dylan Cooper
4. Tawni
5. Zora
6. Nico
7. Marshall Pike
8. So Random!
9. Orlando
10. Mackenzie Falls